D1551440

Revealing the Kingdom
A Look at the Kingdom Parables

Gary C. Hampton

Springridge Publishing
P.O. Box 905
Clinton, MS 39060
www.springridgebooks.com

.

CONTENTS

INTRODUCTION

The word parable actually comes from two Greek words. *Para* means beside. *Ballein* means I throw, or I place. Thus, we have to throw or place beside. In parables, Jesus, and other inspired men, laid stories that would be familiar to their listeners alongside spiritual truths. The people who were receptive to God's teaching could then learn something of God's will.

When it comes to man understanding God's plan for a spiritual kingdom, parables are specially suited to man's need. Over the course of several lessons, it will be our purpose to learn about Christ's kingdom by studying his parables. Numerous works were consulted to write these lessons, with two being of special interest. *Lessons from the Parables* by Neil Lightfoot (Grand Rapids: Baker Book House, 1965) and J. W. McGarvey and Philip Y. Pendleton's *The Fourfold Gospel* (Cincinnati: The Standard Publishing Foundation). The reader is encouraged to read these works to discover other important lessons.

The Lord delivered more parables directly dealing with the kingdom than can be easily handled in a quarterly study. For that reason, three parables have been put in Appendix 1, 2 and 3 at the end of the thirteen week study.

Gary C. Hampton

LESSON 1:
HEARING AND DOING
Matthew 7:21-27; Luke 6:46-49

Anyone who has ever been a student or taught a student knows that listening is much easier than doing. Parents learn early in their children's lives that they can "hear" what is said without really "hearing." Children assure them that they have been heard, but no action arises from the hearing. The Lord saw that problem and warned against it in at least two parables.

"Lord, Lord" Is Not Enough

Jesus knew some would call upon his name yet refuse to yield to his authority by obeying the Father's will. He knew there would be those in the judgment day who would claim to have taught and done great works in his name yet would still have to hear the Lord say, "I never knew you; depart from Me, you who practice lawlessness!" (Matt. 7:21-23).

There have been those who worked for God but totally rejected his will at some time in their lives. Aaron served as Moses' mouthpiece before the people and Pharaoh. Yet, that first high priest was also guilty of taking the people's gold and molding it into a calf for the children of Israel to sinfully worship. Balaam knew he could not curse God's people, but taught Balak how to bring God's wrath upon them by tempting them to sin. Judas walked with the Lord, but was able to sell him for thirty pieces of silver. Hymenaeus and Alexander rejected the faith and a good conscience, thereby suffering shipwreck, and Demas forsook Paul.

The Parable of the Builders

Jesus told those assembled on the mount that he was going to tell them what a man who heard his words and did what he said would be like. Then, he told of a man who dug down until he found rock upon which to place the foundation of his house. Boles tells us, "The hills of Palestine were subject to heavy rainstorms at certain seasons of the year, and consequently to floods; water rushing down the ravines would soon undermine the foundation, if the house was not built on a rock." Of course, if it was built on a rock, it was safe, just as surely as the man who hears and obeys the will of God is safe.

In contrast, the Lord said the man who heard his word but refused to do the Father's will would be like a man who thoughtlessly built his house on the sand. There are numerous gullies in Palestine which have been formed in the ravines by the rushing waters of the rainy season. They are flat and very inviting to one in a hurry to build during the dry season. Unfortunately, when the rains return, a house built on the sand is soon undermined and swept away in the floods (Matt. 7:24-27).

Lessons from the Parable

The greatest lesson of this parable is the importance of hearing and doing. When Jesus taught his disciples the lesson on humble service, he said, "If you know these things, happy are you if you do them" (John 13:17). Our Lord also said, "If you love Me, keep

My commandments." Later, he added, "You are My friends if you do whatever I command you" (John 14:15; 15:14). In Luke 8:19-21, when they told Jesus his mother and brethren were waiting to see him outside, he responded by saying, "My mother and My brothers are these who hear the word of God and do it."

Lightfoot also used the parable to gain insight into our failure to respond to the things we hear. There are those who do not act because they delay their action. After some time has passed, the urgency of responding also passes. Perhaps that is why Paul said, "See then that you walk circumspectly, not as fools but as wise, redeeming the time, because the days are evil" (Eph. 5:15-16). Others, like the man in a hurry to find a flat place to build his house, do not want to be required to do too much to follow Christ. Still others, like the foolish builder in the dry season, do not look ahead to the possible rains and floods in the future. They choose to wait, like Felix, for a "convenient time" (Acts 24:25).

Lightfoot further noted that times of testing are sure to come. In the parable, it was the rains, winds and floods. In our lives, it can be any number of tragedies, such as losing a job, illness, an erring child, divorce or death. It is important to build our lives on the solid foundation of Christ and obedience to his will so that we can withstand the tests!

Note: Appendix 1 is a lesson on the second parable on hearing.

Discussion Questions

1. What does the word "parable" mean? How did inspired men use such stories?

2. Why is it not enough to call on Jesus as Lord? Give examples to illustrate your point.

3. Briefly tell about the parable and describe the people the two builders represent.

4. What was the lesson Jesus was trying to teach?

5. What actions could you take to avoid being a foolish builder?

LESSON 2:
GARMENTS, WINSEKINS, AND WINE
Matthew 9:14-17; Mark 2:18-22; Luke 5:33-39

A Question About Fasting

The disciples of John, along with the Pharisees and their scribes according to Luke, asked Jesus why his disciples did not fast. One can understand the question since John had taught his disciples to fast and the Pharisees had two regular weekly fasts on Monday and Thursday (compare Luke 18:11-12). Also, it might be noted that John the Baptist was continually on a diet of locusts and wild honey, which might have been viewed by some as almost a continual fast (Matt. 3:4).

In contrast, the disciples of Jesus were never observed fasting and, on this occasion, they were in the midst of feasting. It would seem, at least for John's disciples, that the question was an honest one. Jesus used four parables to answer their question.

The Friends of the Bridegroom

Among the Jews, it was customary for the groom and his family to hold a feast in association with his wedding (Judg. 14:10-11; Matt. 22:1-4; Luke 14:8; John 2:1-11). The feast would serve as a period of joyous celebration over the impending marital union of the couple. As long as the bride and groom were present, it would have been totally inappropriate for his friends to fast, since such is often coupled with mourning (2 Sam. 12:15-17). If the groom were taken away from the feast because of sickness, accident or death, then, they might have fasted, but never while he was with them!

Jesus used the very familiar story of a wedding feast to illustrate the nature of his relationship with his disciples. He was sent by God to be the groom to a new bride, the church (compare Eph. 5:22-33). As long as Jesus was with his disciples bodily, they would not fast. However, he did indicate there would come a time, after his departure, when his disciples would fast. It should be noted that Jesus prescribed no specific fast days for those who would be a part of his kingdom, or church, but he did believe they would have occasion for fasting (Matt. 9:14-15). It would also be good to pause long enough to realize Jesus understood, even at this early date in his ministry, that he would be violently taken away from his disciples and they would have a reason to be sorrowful.

New Cloth and an Old Garment

Jesus next pictures an individual with a tear in an old garment. He states that no one would use a new piece of cloth, which had never been shrunk, to repair such a tear. If he did, it would shrink during the first washing and make the tear in the old garment much

6

worse than it had been originally.

It is likely that many of those who followed Jesus thought of him as a reformer of Judaism. If they understood this illustration, they would have seen he did not come to repair the old garment of Judaism, but to make a new garment. If the Pharisees' rules about fasting had harmed God's intent for the law of Moses, Jesus did not intend to put new cloth over the hole to repair the garment (Matt. 9:16).

New Wines and Old Wineskins

Similarly, Jesus stated that men did not put new wine into old wineskins. The reason was obvious to all his listeners. It was common at the time of Jesus' life on earth for men to store wine in skins, usually the hide of a goat. If one did put new wine into old wineskins, when the new wine began to ferment, and thereby expand, it would burst the old wineskins and the wine would be lost. Fresh skins were used because they still retained an elasticity which would allow for expansion of the fermenting wine (Matt. 9:17).

Jesus was clearly saying that it would never do to put the new gospel into the old Jewish law. The law of Moses would have been torn apart if Christ's law had been inserted in its middle. There would have been conflict between remembering the Sabbath day to keep it holy and commemorating Christ's death on the Lord's day. Animal sacrifices commanded under Moses' law would have been a waste of time after the death of Christ.

God did not intend for his Son to modify the existing law, but fulfill it, take it out of the way and establish a new covenant with his chosen people (Matt. 5:17-18; Col. 2:14; Heb. 8:7-13; 9:15-17). It was, then, completely proper for Jesus' disciples to ignore the traditional fasts of the Pharisees and rejoice during the time the promised Messiah, or bridegroom, was with them!

Old Wine and New

Finally, Jesus said a man who had tasted old wine would not want to drink new wine. This may have indicated the Pharisees would not be very receptive to the gospel. They had been drinking in the old wine of the law of Moses all of their lives. They had come to enjoy the position of power they had under that system. Therefore, they would not be receptive to the new ideas presented by God's Spokesman for the last days (Luke 5:39; Heb. 1:1-4).

Discussion Questions

1. What led to John's disciples and the Pharisees asking about fasting?

2. Compare the traditional wedding feast of Jesus' day to the purpose of fasting.

3. Why would one not put new cloth over a tear in an old garment? Explain how this relates to the gospel.

4. What was Jesus' point in the illustration of new wine in old wineskins?

5. In your own words, tell the parable of the man who had drunken old wine. What is the point of this parable?

Gary C. Hampton

LESSON 3:
MEN'S HEARTS PROVIDE SOIL FOR THE KINGDOM SEED
Matthew 13:1-23; Mark 4:1-25; Luke 8:4-18

The Parable of the Sower

When Jesus came out of a house (Mark 3:19), he sat down to teach a multitude beside the Sea of Galilee. The first parable he told on that day was about a farmer who went out to his field to sow seed. A portion of that seed fell on the wayside, or foot path. Palestine in the days of Christ was a land without fences. People walking through an area naturally followed basically the same path. Eventually, there was a hard, packed way to follow through the fields. Seed which fell on this ground would either be trampled underfoot or eaten by the birds.

Other seed fell on rocky ground. This was a rock ledge covered by a small layer of topsoil. Seed on such ground would readily spring up. However, because its roots could not go deep, the plant soon withered. Some of the seed fell on ground already covered with thorns. The thorns would compete with the young seedling for sun and moisture. At last, the thorns would choke the seedling to death. Seed also fell on good ground. Harvest time found such ground yielding thirty, sixty or one hundred times as much grain as was originally sown.

The Importance of Learning from the Parables

Jesus called for those who could hear his message to seek for an understanding of its meaning. Parables were intended by our Lord to uncover that which had been hidden. The word "mystery" is used in the New Testament to refer to the plan of God for the redemption of man which had been hidden from previous generations (compare Rom. 16:25-27).

Of course, parables were also intended to hide the truth from those who were not ready to receive such. To them, the stories told would be innocent little stories of common life. Interestingly, Paul says the rulers of this world would not have crucified Jesus if they had fully understood the mystery (1 Cor. 2:6-8). Jesus promised those who had receptive hearts would find the parables teaching them much more about the kingdom of heaven. Those who had little understanding and refused to receive more would find the parables presenting them with a maze which obscured understanding.

All of this was in accord with the prophecy of Isaiah 6:9-10. The Lord pronounced a blessing on all those who saw and actually perceived the truth revealed in the parables. Others had longed to see the fullness of the truth but had not been given the same opportunity (1 Pet. 1:10-12).

Explaining the Parable of the Sower

Christ used this parable to point out the responsibility an individual has when he hears. The seed of the kingdom is God's word. The sower is someone who preaches the word. The four soils represent different conditions of the human heart.

The wayside soil represents the person who has closed his mind completely to the word of God (Heb. 3:12-13). The rocky soil represents the person who fails to think out carefully what he has heard. He does not follow through completely and develops no depth of understanding. So, when hard times come, he abandons the truth. The thorny-soiled heart is that individual who loves the cares and pleasures of this life more than God's kingdom. They allow such to choke God's word out of their life. The good soil represents the person who understands, receives and keeps with patience the word of God.

Applying the Parable of the Sower

Reception of the gospel and the fruit it produces depends upon the heart of the one who receives it. The real hearer is the man who listens, who understands and who obeys. "But be doers of the word, and not hearers only, deceiving yourselves" (James 1:22). We must, therefore, be sure our minds are open and receptive to the word of God.

Teachers also need to remember it is their job to sow the seed without regard to the types of soil it falls upon. Each one who proclaims the gospel must recognize God is the one who will give the increase (1 Cor. 3:5-7; Isaiah 55:10-11). God expects every faithful Christian to sow the seed of the kingdom (2 Tim. 2:2; Mark 16:15-16). We cannot be faithful and be quiet!

Gary C. Hampton

Discussion Questions

1. What was Jesus' stated purpose for using parables?

2. Briefly relate the parable of the sower.

3. What can the parables help us learn?

4. Name the four types of soil and what each represents.

5. What lessons can we learn from the parable of the sower?

Gary C. Hampton

LESSON 4:
HARVESTING THE SONS OF THE KINGDOM
Matthew 13:24-30, 36-43

The Parable of the Wheat and the Tares

Jesus compared the kingdom of heaven to a man sowing good seed in a field. While he was resting at night, an enemy sowed tares in the field. Lightfoot thinks the tares are of the variety known as "bearded darnel." It was a poisonous rye grass which looks very much like wheat in its early stages of development. When the wheat began to put on heads, it was obvious tares were mixed in with the wheat.

Rather than damage the wheat by trying to separate the tares, the householder instructed his servants to let both grow together. He planned to let the reapers bundle up the tares to be burned and collect the wheat in his barn.

Jesus Explained the Meaning

No better interpreter for any parable could be found than the Lord. The disciples asked him what the parable meant. He said the one who sowed the seed was the Son of Man. The world was the field. The good seed were members of the church, or children of the

17

kingdom. The tares were children of the devil's kingdom. The devil was the enemy who sowed wicked people in the world. Jesus said the angels would harvest the sons of God and the sons of the devil at the end of the world.

The sons of the devil will be gathered together to be burned. The sons of God, on the other hand, will be taken to a glorious place. They will enjoy the kingdom of their Father.

Christians Confront Sin In the World

Much as some might dream of an exclusively Christian community or nation, the fact is that saints and sinners live in this world together. Jesus prayed, "I have given them your word; and the world has hated them because they are not of the world, just as I am not of the world. I do not pray that you should take them out of the world, but that you should keep them from the evil one" (John 17:14-15).

Christians must constantly be on guard against the temptation to sin. For instance, "those who desire to be rich fall into temptation and a snare, and into many foolish and harmful lusts which drown men in destruction and perdition" (1 Tim. 6:9). Instead of believing they are not subject to sin, Christians should rely on God's help to overcome temptation (1 John 1:7-10; 1 Cor. 10:12-13).

The Devil Has Children Too

The devil sows seed just as surely as the Lord does. Paul describes him as, "the prince of the power of the air, the spirit who now works in the sons of disobedience" (Eph. 2:2). Sinners are truly children of the devil. John says, "He who sins is of the devil, for the devil has sinned from the beginning" (1 John 3:8a).

It should be remembered that it is not always easy to distinguish between the Lord's children and the devil's. In Paul's day, some false teachers pretended to be apostles of Christ. "And no wonder! For Satan himself transforms himself into an angel of light. Therefore it is no great thing if his ministers also transform themselves into ministers of righteousness, whose end will be according to their works" (2 Cor. 11:12-15).

In the sermon on the mount, Jesus even described some who would call him Lord yet not do the will of the Father in heaven. He says such will not be allowed to enter into the kingdom of heaven. "Many will say to Me in that day, 'Lord, Lord, have we not prophesied in Your name, cast out demons in Your name, and done many wonders in Your name?' And then I will declare to them, 'I never knew you; depart from Me, you who practice lawlessness" (Matt. 7:21-23).

The Lord Will Judge

The parable makes it plain that it is not the job of any Christian to determine the final destiny of others. Instead, God and the angels will separate all people into two groups. The sons of the devil will be cast into the fire. The sons of God will be invited into the kingdom of heaven for eternity (John 5:28-29; Gal. 6:7-8; Rev. 20:13-15).

Jesus warned his followers not to judge so they would not be judged. Christians should not focus on the faults and sins of others. Instead, they should rid their own lives of sin so they might please God. It is only their responsibility to observe the fruits another's life produces to determine if they are false prophets. If so, they should be avoided. However, even the false prophet can only ultimately be condemned by God (Matt. 7:15, 15-20).

Discussion Questions

1. Briefly tell the parable of the wheat and tares.

2. Explain the meaning as given by the Lord.

3. What facts are apparent about the Christian in relation to sin?

4. What observations do you have concerning Satan's children?

5. Why should Christians not judge others? What role should fruit inspection play in the life of a Christian? Why?

LESSON 5:
THE GROWTH OF THE KINGDOM
Matthew 13:31-33; Mark 4:30-32; Luke 13:18-21

The Kingdom Grows Like a Mustard Seed

McGarvey suggests the mustard seed is the smallest of all seeds sown in a garden. Yet, in the area where Christ was speaking, it grows to a height of ten feet. In fact, the bush is as large as some trees in the region. Birds use the branches of these bushes to build their nests.

Jesus likened the remarkable growth of the mustard seed to that of the kingdom. Its humble beginnings are found in the birth of a child lain in a manger in the tiny town of Bethlehem. Instead of the king being announced with a fanfare of trumpets, a man dressed in camel skins and eating locusts and wild honey proclaimed the kingdom was at hand. Vast armies with shining armor did not march out against the armies of other nations to conquer huge tracts of land. Just twelve men were charged with going into all the world and preaching the gospel (Matt. 2:1; Luke 2:17; Mark 1:18; 16:15-16).

Yet, on the first Pentecost after Christ's resurrection, about three thousand souls were added to their number. After Peter and John preached in the temple, the number of men who believed came to near five thousand. Later, because of daily preaching in the temple and every house, the number of the disciples was said to be multiplying. After the apostles dealt quickly and effectively with the problem of daily ministering to the Hellenist widows, Luke states, "the number of the disciples multiplied greatly in Jerusalem, and a great many of the priests were obedient to the faith" (Acts 2:41; 4:4;

6:1, 7). Truly, the kingdom grew to great proportions from a small beginning! Paul was actually able to say the gospel had been preached in the whole world (Col. 1:23).

The Kingdom Grows Like Leaven Spreads

A cook in Christ's day who needed leaven could not run to the grocery store and buy some. Instead, a lump of leavened dough was saved from each baking. It was added to some more meal to ferment. Leaven is used by inspired men to represent the negative working of false teachers and sin in some passages (Mark 8:15; 1 Cor. 5:6; Gal. 5:9).

However, in the parable of the woman hiding leaven in three measures of meal it represents the spread of the church. McGarvey says, "Leaven represents the quickness, quietness, thoroughness and sureness with which gospel truth diffuses itself through human society."

Lessons Learned from the Spread of Leaven

Neil R. Lightfoot suggests three properties of leaven the Christian should note. First, leaven can only work if it is in the dough. Similarly, Christian influence will only have an impact on the world if we are living exemplary lives (Phil. 2:14-16; 1 Pet. 3:15-16). Also, the gospel can only work if one allows it into his heart (compare Mark 4:20; Luke 8:15; Acts 2:41; Rev. 3:20).

Second, leaven has the ability to change things. It changed a persecutor of Christians into a preacher of the gospel (Acts 26:9-11; 9:17-22). Obedience to the gospel causes God to translate one from the kingdom of darkness to the kingdom of Christ. A man's goals will be changed from temporal to eternal. The gospel will make a man change from sinful to righteous acts (Col. 1:13; 3:1-17). He will be a new creature. The man of sin will be put away and he will live a new life (2 Cor. 5:17; Rom. 6:3-4).

Third, leaven is contagious. When Andrew was invited to follow Jesus, he first found his brother, Peter, and invited him to come along. Philip went to find his friend, Nathanael, to urge him to come see the one who he believed Moses and the prophets had written about (John 1:35-51). The angel of God told Cornelius to send for Peter so he could be told what he must do. When Peter arrived in Caesarea, he found "Cornelius was waiting for them, and had called together his relatives and close friends" (Acts 10:1-24). Paul felt compelled to preach the gospel to all who would listen (1 Cor. 9:16).

Leaven Is Disturbing

Lightfoot also commented on leaven's ability to disturb things with which it comes in contact. Anyone who has seen the fermenting process knows leaven disturbs the meal with all sorts of bubbling and working. The gospel likewise disturbs men. Some at Philippi took Paul and Silas to the magistrates, saying, "These men, being Jews, exceedingly trouble our city; and they teach customs which are not lawful for us, being Romans, to receive or observe" (Acts 16:20-21). In Thessalonica, others said, "These who have turned the world upside down have come here too" (17:6).

Interestingly, this disturbance arises from the working of each particle of leaven. Boles wrote, "The leaven, hid in meal, diffuses itself by its very nature, pressing evermore outward from one particle to another till it permeates the whole mass." For the church to reach all the lost with the truth, each member must press outward toward those friends and neighbors who have not yet heard the good news (2 Tim. 2:2; Luke 24:46-47)!

David Lipscomb challenges the thinking of the church. "Leaven is an active working principle. It may be an active working principle of good, or it may be an active principle of evil. Place either in an inactive mass, it will leaven the whole mass into a good or bad working mass." He went on to say, "The church often becomes an inactive, lifeless mass. A leaven of good or evil working and spreading in the church will work for good or evil and leaven the whole church for good or evil." For that reason, Christians need to be constantly encouraging one another to "love and good works" (Heb. 10:24).

Discussion Questions

1. Describe the nature of the growth of a mustard seed.

2. What facts support the Lord's comparison of church growth to that of a mustard seed?

3. Give three characteristics of the spread of leaven and explain how the growth of the kingdom is similar.

4. Give some New Testament examples of the gospel's disturbing influence.

5. If the church becomes an inactive mass, what should concerned Christians do?

Gary C. Hampton

LESSON 6:
THE VALUE OF THE KINGDOM
Matthew 13:44-46

The Hidden Treasure and Pearl of Great Price

The two parables we are considering today are short and simple, yet powerful. In the first, a man found a treasure in a field. He then hid it and went to buy the field so he could possess the treasure. During Jesus' time, it was common for one to hide treasure in the ground for safe keeping. If the one who hid it died, the treasure's whereabouts might not be known.

Some have suggested the hiding of the treasure was unethical. However, Edersheim in *The Life and Times of Jesus The Messiah* says, "It was, at least, in entire accordance with Jewish law...The law went so far as to adjudge to the purchaser of fruits anything found among these fruits."

In the second, a merchant was seeking beautiful pearls. When he found one of great value, he sold everything he had to be able to buy it. While the man who found the treasure in the field likely did so by accident, this merchant knew he was looking for valuable pearls.

The truth can be found in a manner quite accidental or very intentionally. McGarvey suggests the Samaritan woman was one of the former and the Ethiopian Eunuch one of the latter (John 4; Acts 8). It does not matter how one finds it as long as he recognizes its

29

potential and gives up all to possess it.

The Supreme Value of the Kingdom

The kingdom of God is worth more than all other possessions. Its value can be seen in the purchase price Jesus paid. Paul said Christ gave his own blood (Acts 20:28). One can see the worth of the kingdom by comparing the greatest possible wealth with losing one's soul. In Matthew 16:26, Jesus asked his disciples, "For what is a man profited if he gains the whole world, and loses his own soul? Or what will a man give in exchange for his soul?"

Knowing the value of the kingdom should motivate one to seek it as the top priority in his life. "But seek first the kingdom of God and His righteousness, and all these things shall be added to you" (Matt. 6:33). The Lord had noted the importance of following God as one's only master because divided loyalty would cause one to fail (verse 24).

Sacrificing All to Possess It

Once one realizes the true value of the kingdom, he will have an unquenchable desire to possess it. In fact, he will sacrifice all else to have the kingdom in his life. "Then Jesus said to His disciples, 'If anyone desires to come after Me, let him deny himself, and take up his cross, and follow me. For whoever desires to save his life will lose it, and whoever loses his life for My sake will find it" (Matt. 16:24-25).

Paul described himself as a Jew of the highest standing. "But what things were gain to me, these I have counted loss for Christ. But indeed I also count all things loss for the excellence of the knowledge of Christ Jesus my Lord, for whom I have suffered the loss of all things, and count them as rubbish, that I may gain Christ" (Phil. 3:7-8). He urged the brethren at Rome to present their bodies as living sacrifices which would be acceptable to God (12:12).

The Joy of Possessing the Kingdom

The man who found the hidden treasure reacted in a noteworthy way. "And for joy over it he goes and sells all that he has and buys that field." We have already seen that Paul gave up much to be a part of Christ's kingdom. Yet, he could write in Philippians 4:4, "Rejoice in the Lord always. Again I will say, rejoice!" He learned contentment in times of abasement or plenty. Want did not dissuade him from joy because he could do all things through Christ who strengthened him (4:10-13). One can rejoice in giving up all else because he has found something of ultimate value!

Perhaps the pearl merchant of Christ's story gives us insight into the source of joy. He had a single purpose. When he found the object of that purpose, all else was surrendered to obtain the pearl. Again, Paul shows us the way when he describes his own thinking. "Brethren, I do not count myself to have apprehended; but one thing I do, forgetting those things which are behind and reaching forward to those things which are ahead, I press toward the goal for the prize of the upward call of God in Christ Jesus" (Phil. 3:13-14).

If we would experience the ultimate joy, we must focus on the single goal of heaven. Like the Eunuch, those finding the will of God will not want to be hindered in their obedience. Once such is completed, they too will go on their way rejoicing (Acts 8:26-39).

Discussion Questions

1. What facts make the kingdom of God valuable to you?

2. What does Jesus say one must do to possess the kingdom?

3. List some of the things Paul gave up to be a Christian.

4. What caused the man who gave up all and purchased a field to rejoice? Why do you think one should rejoice upon finding the kingdom of heaven?

5. What special insight does the pearl merchant give us into the truest source of joy?

Gary C. Hampton

LESSON 7:
THE KINGDOM AND THE JUDGMENT
Matthew 13:47-50

Many today would rather treat the judgment as a product of someone's overactive imagination. They do not want to consider the prospect of facing an eternity separated from God's love. Yet, our Lord makes it clear that men will one day be separated into two groups, the good and the bad. The good will be kept in the presence of God's love. The bad will be cast away from God.

The Parable of the Dragnet

Fishermen in Christ's day used a seine net. It sucked up all kinds of fish in its path. The fisherman would then pull the net up on the shore and sort the various fish. There were two types of fish, those good for eating and all others. The good fish were placed in vessels, taken to market and sold. The others were thrown away.

Jesus briefly explained the parable. He said it was describing the events at the end of the age. The angels would be sent forth to separate the wicked from the just. The wicked would be cast into a furnace of fire where there would be wailing and gnashing of teeth.

Striving To Be Among the Good

Clearly, every Christian should set a goal of being found among the good the Lord will keep. Paul wrote, "Test all things; hold fast what is good" (1 Thes. 5:21). The man who would be an elder must be "a lover of what is good." Older women are to be teachers of good things, specifically teaching younger women to be "good." Titus and other young men were to show themselves "to be a pattern of good works." Jesus "gave himself for us, that he might redeem us from all iniquity, and purify unto himself a peculiar people, zealous of good works (Titus 1:8; 2:3, 5, 7,14).

Paul warned, "Do not be deceived: 'Evil company corrupts good habits.'" John said, "Beloved, do not imitate what is evil, but what is good. He who does good is of God, but he who does evil has not seen God." Ultimately, "Who is he who will harm you if you become followers of what is good?" Others may say one is an evil person but their good way of life in Christ will make them ashamed (1 Cor. 15:33; 3 John 11; 1 Pet. 3:13, 16).

Being Found With the Good In the Judgment

The Christian's final goal should be to be separated into the group of good people in the day of judgment. "Having your conversation honest among the Gentiles: that, whereas they speak against you as evildoers, they may by your good works, which they shall behold, glorify God in the day of visitation." A part of the purpose of such good deeds would obviously be to receive a good reward from the Lord (1 Pet. 2:12; Eph. 6:8).

Paul says everyone will appear before Christ's judgment seat to receive a reward according to what he did in the body (2 Cor. 5:10). His words were consistent with the Lord's teachings. "Do not marvel at this; for the hour is coming in which all who are in the graves will hear His voice and come forth--those who have done good, to the resurrection of life, and those who have done evil, to the resurrection of condemnation" (John 5:28-29).

The Furnace of Fire

If people do not want to consider the possibility of coming judgment, they surely do not want to think of impending punishment. Yet, the Lord speaks of a "furnace of fire." That it is a real fire is seen in his statement that "there shall be wailing and gnashing of teeth."

The fire will be for the chaff and those who do not bring forth good fruit. Jesus warned his disciples to cast aside those things that offended them lest they should enter hell's fire with that offending member. He described the fire as everlasting "where 'their worm does not die and the fire is not quenched.'" Of course, it was never intended for man but for the devil and his angels (Matt. 3:12; 7:19; 18:8-9; 25:41; Mark 9:46, 48).

Paul told the brethren at Thessalonica, "when the Lord Jesus is revealed from heaven with His mighty angels, in flaming fire taking vengeance on those who do not know God, and on those who do not obey the gospel of our Lord Jesus Christ. These shall be punished with everlasting destruction from the presence of the Lord and from the glory of His power." Through John, Jesus delivered a revelation to reassure those suffering Christians of the first century.

He said the devil would be cast into the lake of fire and brimstone. He also said those whose names were not found written in the book of life would be cast into the lake of fire. Then, he listed those types of sin which would consign one to the lake burning with fire and brimstone, which is the second death (2 Thes. 1:79; Rev. 20:10, 14-15; 21:8).

No doubt, hell is real. The Lord told us those things we must do to be counted among the good. We should strive to be among that number the angels will separate to be with their Lord in eternity!

Discussion Questions

1. What did Jesus say the parable of the dragnet meant?

2. What can you do to help others and yourself be found among the good?

3. What things can prevent you from being among the good?

4. List some of the things you know about the judgment.

5. Describe hell and list some of those who will spend eternity there.

LESSON 8:
FORGIVENESS AND THE KINGDOM
Matthew 18:15-35

The Christian's Response to Others' Sins Against Him

In the normal course of human relations, one brother will sin against another. Jesus prescribed that the offended brother should go to the one who sinned against him in an effort to restore his brother. Edersheim tells us this was in stark contrast to the teaching of the Jewish rabbis. They said the offending party must make an effort to correct the problem in the presence of witnesses. Sometimes, they even required such to be repeated three times. Obviously, their concern was not for the condition of the offender. Instead, they practiced a form of humiliation. Of course, if the offending party was aware of the offense, he too was obligated to correct the problem (Matt. 5:23-24).

Even if the brother was not restored in the first approach, Jesus directed his followers to take one or two others with him. They could help deal with the matter in an effort to restore the brother. The loving way to handle the matter focused on gaining the lost brother. It was only after taking the matter to the church, without success, that the brother was to be treated as one who refused the knowledge of God.

"How Often Shall My Brother Sin Against Me, And I Forgive Him?"

Peter's response to the Lord's instruction makes it clear he did not understand the heart of love. The rabbis taught "forgiveness should not be extended more than three times," according to Edersheim. So, Peter probably thought he was being generous when he asked if he should forgive his brother up to seven times. However, Jesus' answer shows he was more concerned with his disciples having the type of loving heart that could truly forgive. Then, numbering offenses would be out of the question.

Actually, the bounds of a Christian's forgiveness should be the same as the bounds to God's forgiveness. After all, those who would be children of God must strive to exhibit the love of their Father (Matt. 5:43-48). Such thinking is apparently behind the parable Jesus went on to tell.

The Marvelous Grace of God!

The King in this parable stands for God. He called in his servants to settle accounts. One was brought before him who owed 10,000 talents. A talent weighed approximately one hundred thirty-one pounds in gold and one hundred seventeen pounds in silver. In other words, the debt owed by the servant was 1.17 million pounds of silver, minimum! With twelve troy ounces to a pound and an ounce going for even $3, the total debt is a staggering $42,120,000!

Edersheim well said, "We are debtors to our heavenly King, Who has entrusted to us the administration of what is His, and which we have purloined or misused, incurring an unspeakable debt, which we can never discharge." He went on to say, "But, if in humble repentance we cast ourselves at His Feet, He is ready, in infinite compassion, not only to release us from meet punishment, but O blessed revelation of the Gospel! to forgive us the debt."

God's wonderful love for mankind can be seen in the king's willingness to forgive such a great debt. The singer of Israel proclaimed, "As far as the east is from the west, so far has He removed our transgressions from us." Thus, he told his people, "O Israel, hope in the Lord; for with the Lord there is mercy, and with Him is abundant redemption" (Psa. 103:12; 130:7). God is willing to take the deep stain of sin and remove it if we will but obey. To those who are willing to repent and be changed by baptism into a new man, he has promised a complete blotting out of sin. To those in Christ who confess, he promises faithfully to forgive (Acts 3:19; 1 John 1:9).

The Unmerciful Servant

The servant did not appreciate fully what the king had done for him. Such can be seen in his finding a fellow servant who owed him the equivalent of $70 and demanding payment. His fellow servant made the same appeal he had made to the king. Yet, he would not even give him time to come up with the money but cast him into debtors' prison.

His fellow servants' shock at his actions is seen in their reporting the incident to the king. Here was a man who truly could not recognize the beam just removed from his own eye by the mercy of the king. He has now gone forth to remove the speck in his fellow servant's eye (Matt. 7:15). Instead of condemning, he should have been forgiving. After all, those who would be forgiven by God must be forgiving (Matt. 6:12, 14-15). Paul told the Ephesian brethren, "And be kind to one another, tenderhearted, forgiving one another, just as God in Christ also forgave you" (4:32).

God's Response to the Unforgiving Heart

When the King heard what had happened, he was angry. He expected his servant to imitate his forgiveness. Because he had not, the master restored his original debt and delivered him to the torturers until he had repaid the whole debt. Imagine the unending goal of repaying such a debt from within prison walls! It would be an eternal process filled with suffering.

Jesus stated, "So My heavenly Father also will do to you if each of you, from his heart, does not forgive his brother his trespasses." After all, each of us has sinned in the sight of God. Our sins are worthy of eternal death (Rom. 3:10, 23; 6:23). Yet, God gave the indescribable gift of his own Son's death on Calvary to set us free (2 Cor. 9:15; John 3:16-17)! "All we like sheep have gone astray; we have turned, every one, to his own way; and the Lord has laid on Him the iniquity of us all" (Isa. 53:6). Surely, out of simple gratitude for the release from such a great debt, we should forgive those who sin against us.

Discussion Questions

1. Contrast the worldly versus the Christian response when one sins against another.

2. What mistaken notions do you see in Peter's question about the number of times to forgive?

3. Describe the greatness of your sin debt and God's gracious forgiveness.

4. What made the forgiven servant treat his fellow servant as he did?

5. What facts make it important for us to willingly forgive others?

Gary C. Hampton

LESSON 9:
SEEKING THE LOST
Luke 15:1-32

The Murmuring of the Pharisees and Scribes

Jesus closely associated with sinners, who McGarvey says would be "all who failed to observe the tradition of the elders, and especially their traditional rules of purification. It was not so much the wickedness of this class as their legal uncleanness that made it wrong to eat with them." Such reasoning may have been why Peter withdrew from eating with Gentile converts when some came from James (Gal. 2:11-12).

Jesus also was found in the company of tax collectors, or publicans. The tax collector was most often a man who lived in the district being taxed by the Romans. The Romans usually sold the right to tax within a given district to certain men who would take advantage of the opportunity to profit by overcharging their own countrymen. Sometimes, they even brought false accusations against them. They were therefore considered traitors who plundered their own people for personal gain. Tax collectors were actually classed with the Gentiles, so to eat with them would be viewed as a violation of the law. Jesus' entire purpose in coming to earth was to heal those who were spiritually ill (Luke 5:27-32), so he allowed them to come near to him and learn.

The Pharisees and scribes found such close relationships with people they considered to be unclean to be distasteful. Jesus answered their murmuring by telling three parables about the lost. Each teaches a clear lesson about the Father's view of sinners (Luke 15:1-3).

The Lost Sheep

Sheep were highly valued in Christ's day because they could be used for food, milk, wool and sacrifice (Exo. 12:1-8; Isa. 7:21-22; Job 31:20; Lev. 1:10-11). Shepherds say that sheep are primarily concerned with food and water. If they have those, they will wander aimlessly and possibly end up lost. A man who lost a sheep would leave the others in the place of pasturage and look for the lost. When it was found, the shepherd would lovingly lay it on his shoulders and take it back to the fold rejoicing. Upon his return home, the shepherd would call for his neighbors, who likely knew of the loss and had been concerned with the outcome, to come rejoice with him (Luke 15:4-7).

Men, much like sheep, will wander aimlessly into sin without any regard for the danger if they feel their needs are being met. Despite the fact that they are lost due to their own carelessness, God wants to find the lost. Like the shepherd, he rejoices more over the return of the lost one than over the self-proclaimed righteous who say they have no need for repentance, like the Pharisees (Luke 18:11-12).

The Lost Coin

We may not be impressed when the Lord says a woman had ten coins and lost one, but that was a significant amount of money to the poor working class of Christ's day. In fact, Lightfoot says, "The coin specified by Luke was a Greek *drachma,* which was almost equivalent to a Roman *denarius.*

It was a silver coin, and although worth by our standards less than twenty cents, it was the common wage for a day's labor." When she realized her loss, the woman lit a lamp and began to sweep until it could be found. Their houses were usually without windows, had only one door and a dirt floor which was often covered with dried reeds and rushes, so there were many places for a coin to be hidden.

It would seem the woman's diligent search is again indicative of the love God has for the lost. In this case, it has been noted by some that the coin was likely lost through the negligence of another. Though we would not suggest that anyone is lost because of God's negligence, it does seem that some are influenced in the wrong direction by others. Notice, though the coin may have been lost through another's negligence, it was still considered lost and had to be found! God was so concerned with man's spiritual bondage that he sent his only Son to die and extend the offer of eternal life to those who would express their belief in him through obedience.

The woman rejoiced when the coin was found and invited her neighbors to join her, just as the shepherd who found the sheep had rejoiced. With this simple illustration, Jesus portrayed the heavenly joy over even one sinner who repents (Luke 15:8-10).

The Prodigal

In contrast to the wandering sheep and coin which may have been lost through another's neglect, the prodigal son determined to leave and take his inheritance with him, even before his father died. Since he was the younger brother, one third of his father's goods would ordinarily become his at his father's passing (Deut. 21:17). The prodigal took his future inheritance and wasted it in a far country. When all his money was gone and the country in famine, he attached himself to a certain farmer who sent him out to feed the swine. McGarvey says Jews refused to name pigs and only spoke of them as "*dabhar acheer; i. e.*, 'the other thing,'" so you can imagine the humiliation he felt.

Perhaps the most powerful statement in all of scripture about those lost in sin is, "But when he came to himself." One is not in his right mind when pursuing the course of sin which leads to his eternal destruction. The prodigal was now sufficiently humbled to be ready to go back as a day laborer, which Lightfoot says is the meaning of "hired servants." Though he would not have the security of knowing whether he would have a job from day to day, at least he knew his father treated his servants well! Of course, the father ran to greet him and accepted the penitent back as a son, saying, "for this my son was dead and is alive again; he was lost and is found." Anyone who has felt the terrible burden of his own sins has to rejoice upon hearing those words of the father and noting that he had a party to celebrate his son's return (Luke 15:11-24)!

The Older Brother

It may be remembered that Jesus said the man had two sons. One, the older brother, stayed home with the father the whole time, yet left him in his spirit when he was unwilling to forgive (Rom. 5:6-8; Matt. 6:14-15). He, seemingly, represents the Pharisees and scribes.

Like him, they had many blessings but refused to accept those who had lived in sin and were now returning to God, the heavenly Father.

The older brother's rejection of the father's pleading is reminiscent of the Pharisees' and scribes' unwillingness to acknowledge Jesus as the Christ, the Son of the living God. Still, the father's words to the older son about the recovery of his lost son gives hope to all who have ever recognized their own sinfulness and need for forgiveness (Luke 15:25-32).

Discussion Questions

1. What was a publican? Why do you think Jesus ate with publicans and sinners?

2. Why would a man leave the ninety-nine and seek the one lost sheep?

3. What shows you the value the woman placed on the lost coin?

4. What message for today can be found in Jesus' comment about rejoicing in heaven?

5. What spiritual condition is represented by each of the two sons? What should one do to be sure he is living in the spirit of his Father?

Gary C. Hampton

LESSON 10:
LABORING IN THE KINGDOM
Matthew 19:27-20:16

The Reward for Sacrificial Service

Having heard Jesus' discussion with the rich young ruler, Peter may have been made to wonder about his reward. He commented that he and the rest of the twelve had left all to follow Christ and wondered what reward they would receive. Jesus' immediate response was to speak of the time of the new birth, or regeneration, when he would be on his throne. He said the twelve would also rule at that time over the twelve tribes, or spiritual Israel.

Of course, they reigned with Christ in the sense of reporting his will to men. They even now rule in the writings they left behind. Also, all men who sacrifice for Jesus will be rewarded. Those who have sacrificed family will gain a greater spiritual family. In fact, on one occasion when they told Jesus his mother and brothers were outside he responded in a surprising fashion. "And he stretched out His hand toward His disciples and said, 'Here are My mother and My brothers!'" (Matt. 12:49). The Christian views life in terms of a temporary time on earth followed by eternity (1 Tim. 4:8).

The Invitation to Work in God's Vineyard

At the start of the day, the owner of a vineyard went out to find workers for his vineyard. Those he hired bargained with him for one small coin worth about twenty cents. At the third hour of the workday, or about 9 a.m., he went out and hired more laborers who

54

trusted him to pay them a fair wage for a partial day's work. Then, he hired again at noon, 3 p.m. and even 5 p.m.! Each of these latter went, trusting the owner to give them a fair wage.

It should be noted that the landowner went out repeatedly to seek laborers. The work of the kingdom is ongoing. Laborers are always needed to carry out the works of God. In fact, in this parable, the landowner was still hiring workers at the eleventh hour of a twelve hour work day.

Payment at the End of the Day

The law required payment to be made to each worker at the end of the day. "You shall not defraud your neighbor, nor rob him. The wages of him who is hired shall not remain with you all night until morning," was the instruction of Moses' law as found in Leviticus 19:13.

Deuteronomy 24:15 states it even more clearly, when it says, "Each day you shall give him his wages, and not let the sun go down on it, for he is poor and has set his heart on it; lest he cry out against you to the Lord, and it be sin to you."

When the day was over, the owner called all the workers together and lined them up with the last hired being first paid and the first hired last paid. Not one complaint was heard from those who were trusting the master to pay a fair price. Actually, each received a day's wage for less than a day's work. Only those who worked the whole day, having bargained for a specific sum, were upset. They felt they deserved more, especially compared to those hired at the eleventh hour!

Beware of the Evil Eye

Despite having worked longer than those hired later in the day, those who worked all day were paid according to their bargain. No one had any justification in complaining. After all, the lord's money was his to dispense as he pleased. Yet, some seemed to have been stirred to jealousy. As Lightfoot says, "They simply begrudged the owner's generosity. They murmured not because the lord had deprived them, but because he had been so merciful to the others."

The evil eye, or jealousy, is a sin of the heart. It can corrupt him from within (Mark 7:15-23). "A man with an evil eye hastens after riches, and does not consider that poverty will come upon him" (Prov. 28:22). Under the law of Moses, the seventh year was one for forgiving debts. Some might have been jealous of the money they would lose by loaning money to a poor man in the sixth or seventh years, knowing they would have to forgive whatever remained unpaid. God told them not to be jealous and promised to bless them for the good they did (Deut. 15:7-11).

The First Will Be Last and the Last First

This expression is used immediately before and at the end of the parable. Jesus seemed to be stressing the importance of the heart in working for God. There are two types of workers depicted in the parable. Some worked for the landowner to get what they deserved. The rest labored knowing they would not work a full day and trusting in the one who hired them to give them a fair wage. Notice, the men hired at the eleventh hour, when questioned as to why they had been standing idle all day, said, "Because no one hired us." Clearly, they had a willingness to work, but no opportunity. There is no encouragement here to continually delay accepting the Lord's invitation.

At a different time, Jesus asked his disciples if a master thanked his servants for doing what they were commanded. Then he said, "So likewise you, when you have done all those things which you are commanded, say, 'We are unprofitable servants. We have done what was our duty to do'" (Luke 17:7-10).

Jews who followed Christ early on, the apostles and even some today need to keep this in mind. We are merely doing our duty in serving God. Not one of us can truthfully demand eternal life when we stand at the judgment bar. Instead, we need to exhibit a willingness to work and trust in the Lord to give us a reward far better than we deserve (Matt. 7:21; Rom. 6:23).

Discussion Questions

1. Relate Peter's question and how it fit in with the parable.

2. Name some things people sacrifice to be Christians. What do they gain?

3. What significance do you see in the landowner getting workers throughout the day?

4. Why were some satisfied with their pay? Why were others not satisfied?

5. What was the evil eye of which Christ spoke? How can we avoid it?

6. What type of heart is needed to cause one to be among the last who will be first?

LESSON 11:
HAVING THE KINGDOM TAKEN AWAY
Matthew 21:33-46; Mark 12:1-12; Luke 20:9-18

The Parable of the Wicked Vinedressers

Having already told the religious leaders the publicans and harlots would enter the kingdom before them, Jesus went on to give a parable explaining a part of the reason. In it, the kingdom is compared to a vineyard. The landowner planted and completely equipped a vineyard. He then leased the land to some vinedressers. They agreed to pay the landowner out of the fruit of the vineyard.

When harvest time came, the landowner sent his servants to collect the rent. The vinedressers beat, stoned and killed the multiplied numbers of servants sent to collect. "Therefore still having one son, his beloved, he also sent him to them last, saying, 'They will respect my son.'" However, the wicked vinedressers plotted against the son in hopes of getting his inheritance, which would include the vineyard in which they worked (John 11:47-50). They then cast him out of the vineyard and killed him. It appears this parable is suggesting the Jews knew they were rejecting a special messenger from God when they killed Jesus.

Obviously, this is a reference to the plots against the life of Christ. They finally succeeded in casting him outside the city of Jerusalem and crucifying him (Acts 7:51-52). The writer of Hebrews speaks of this. He makes an apparent reference to the Day of Atonement when the bullock and goat for sin offering were burned outside the camp. Jesus had to die outside Jerusalem because he was an offering for sin (Lev. 16:27; Heb. 13:11-13).

Christ's Question and the Leaders' Answer

Jesus then asked, "Therefore, when the owner of the vineyard comes, what will he do to those vinedressers?" Some of Christ's listeners correctly judged the owner would destroy those men and lease the vineyard to others who would honor their agreement with him. Others, perhaps recognizing the full import of such a conclusion, said "Certainly not!" However, the correct answer was the former.

Their answer exposed the Father's thinking about them. Coffman calls special attention to the fact that the son was sent last. The Jews had rejected a multitude of messengers from God right down to John the baptizer (1 Kings 18:13; 22:24-27; Matt. 14:3-12; Heb. 11:35-38). Jesus is God's last spokesman to sinful man (Heb. 1:12; 2:13). Those who reject him will not receive another messenger from the Father. He waited with patience and longsuffering as they rejected the prophets; then asked his Son to take the form of a servant so he could send him (Phil. 2:5-8). He served as the final messenger and the only fully acceptable sacrifice (Heb. 10:26-31). Since they rejected him, they could only look forward to judgment with fear.

God Foretold The Rejection of Christ

Jesus went on to quote Psalm 118:22-23. He told the religious leaders the kingdom of God would be taken from them and given to a nation which would bear fruit for him. McGarvey says the quotation "is here by Jesus applied as a prophecy to the Pharisees, who, in their treatment of him, were like unskilled builders who reject the very cornerstone of the building which they seek to erect." He went on to say, "They blundered in constructing their theory of the coming kingdom, and could find no room for one such as Jesus in it."

The religious leaders stumbled at the teachings of Christ. They were broken by them in the sense that they were condemned for not accepting him for who he was. "He who believes in Him is not condemned; but he who does not believe is condemned already, because he has not believed in the name of the only begotten Son of God" (John 3:18). When he comes in judgment, those who have not obeyed him will be crushed under the weight of his judgment. "In the day when God will judge the secrets of men by Jesus Christ, according to my gospel" (Rom. 2:16).

Applying the Parable

It is important to make application of this parable to our day. After all, we have been greatly blessed by God. He has provided a wonderful kingdom for us. "He has delivered us from the power of darkness and translated us into the kingdom of the Son of His love, in whom we have redemption through His blood, the forgiveness of sins" (Col. 1:13-14). We have a protective hedge around us in the form of his promise to always provide a way of escape for us (1 Cor. 10:13).

All that he expects in return is our bearing fruit to his glory (John 15:18). We must give him our lives in sacrificial service. "I beseech you therefore, brethren, by the mercies of God, that you present your bodies a living sacrifice, holy, acceptable to God, which is your reasonable service. And do not be conformed to this world, but be transformed by the renewing of your mind, that you may prove what is that good and acceptable and perfect will of God" (Rom. 12:12).

To fail to give God the fruits of our labors is to jeopardize our eternal life with him in heaven. We must be careful not to reject and kill his Son afresh (Heb. 6:4-6). It would actually be better to never have known God's way than to be a part of it and turn back to the ways of the world (2 Pet. 2:20-22). The Father will surely punish those who abuse his last great messenger, Jesus, the Son!

Discussion Questions

1. Describe the blessings of Israel's relationship to God in light of the parable.

2. Explain why Jesus portrayed the son as dying outside of the vineyard.

3. What was the thinking of the Father toward the religious leaders? Why?

4. What verses did Jesus quote? What do they mean?

5. Having seen what happened to the religious leaders, what should we do?

LESSON 12:
THE KINGDOM INVITATION
Matthew 22:1-14; Luke 14:1-24

The Setting

Matthew 21 closed with the elders, scribes, chief priests and Pharisees plotting to kill Jesus. The only thing holding them back was their fear of the multitudes of people who thought Jesus was a prophet. He knew precisely what they were thinking. Chapter 22 opens with Jesus answering thoughts and words they had never expressed in public. He showed them the danger of their attitudes by telling the parable of the wedding feast.

A parable with similar lessons is found in Luke 14:12-24. It was told on a Sabbath day when Jesus was invited into the house of one of the rulers of the Pharisees to eat. The Pharisees watched our Lord closely that day to see if he would do anything they could criticize.

Jesus healed a man with a disease called dropsy. He also taught them to take the lesser, rather than the greater, seats. Then, they would not be embarrassed by being asked to go down to a lower seat. Instead, they would be exalted by being asked to move up to a better seat. He told them to invite those to their feasts who could not invite them to a feast in return. By so doing, they could look forward to being repaid for the good they did in eternity.

The Invitation to the Wedding

Just as we receive wedding invitations days, and even weeks, in advance, so did the people of Jesus' day. They had plenty of time to place the event on their calendar and make plans to attend. Jesus also knew the invitation to a banquet was extended days in advance. The exact day would be set, with the time to be determined as the final meal preparations were made. Then, when everything was ready, the one giving the banquet would send for the invited guests.

Similarly, the Jews had been told of the coming Messiah for years. God and the prophets had been speaking and writing of this king and his kingdom since the beginning of time (Gen. 3:15; Deut. 18:15; Isa. 9:6-7; Dan. 2:36-45). There was no reason for the Jews to be unprepared for the Lord's entrance into the world.

Also, Jesus has told his disciples that he has gone to prepare a place for them. He has promised to come again to receive those who are his own (John 14:16). We do not know the exact day of his coming, so we must be watchful (Matt. 24:36-39; 2 Pet. 3:10).

The Man Without a Wedding Garment

When the king came in, he observed a man who did not have on a wedding garment. The king asked him how he came to be there without wearing the proper garment. McGarvey says the fact that the man was speechless shows he was without excuse. So, we know he had access to the appropriate garment but did not wear it. He was responsible for his own lack of preparation (compare Matt. 25:1-13).

It would seem this guest represents those who have accepted the gospel call but choose not to live in accord with the Lord's will. Demas would be an example of one who worked on the Lord's side but later abandoned it for worldly pursuits (Col. 4:14; Phile. 24; 2 Tim. 4:10). Paul warned those Gentile Christians who considered being circumcised to please God that such would cause them to be under the law of Moses and fallen from grace (5:14). It is possible to accept Christ's invitation yet be cast into outer darkness for failing to wear the proper garment (Eph. 4:17-24).

"Many Are Called, But Few Are Chosen"

Christ's conclusion, "For many are called, but few are chosen," ought to give all pause. It can truly be said the gospel invitation is for all (Matt. 11:28-30; Rev. 22:17). "Then Peter opened his mouth and said: 'In truth I perceive that God shows no partiality. But in every nation whoever fears Him and works righteousness is accepted by Him'" (Acts 10:34-35).

The gospel's power to save is not limited to a particular people. God wants all men in every location to be saved (Rom. 1:16; 1 Tim. 2:4). Thus, Jesus sent his disciples into all the world with the saving message. Anyone who believes and puts on Christ in penitent baptism will be saved from his past sins (Matt. 28:18-20; Mark 16:15-16; Luke 24:46-48).

The trouble is, not all will accept the invitation. Some, like the first guests invited to the marriage of the king's son, make light of God's call. Others have beaten, persecuted and killed his messengers. Because of their refusal, they will be barred from the wonderful feast in God's eternal kingdom.

Excuses Will Not Be Accepted

We may try to rationalize why we are not responding as God would have us to, but our excuses will not be accepted. In the parable of the wedding feast, one went to his farm and another to his business. In the parable of the great supper, one said he had to look at a piece of land he had bought. One wonders why he bought it sight unseen. Another said he had to test five yoke of oxen he had purchased. He cared more for business, which could have been delayed, than the feast with his friend since he set this proving on the very day it took place. A third used a new bride as an excuse. The marriage had already taken place and had no special attendant duties. So, he placed his relationship with his wife, which apparently was not in jeopardy, above honoring a commitment to his friend.

Both parables show us the urgency of responding to the Lord's invitation. Nothing can be put above it lest we find we cannot accept it at a later time. It is imperative that we let nothing hinder our obedience to the Lord!

Discussion Questions

1. What lessons can we learn from Jesus' teachings on the higher and lower seats?

2. Why should we be preparing for the Lord's return? How urgently?

3. What lessons can Christians learn from the man with no wedding garment?

4. List some of the various types of people who accepted the gospel call in the New Testament.

5. List some of the excuses given today for not serving. Do you think God will accept them?

LESSON 13:
THOSE WHO WERE READY
Matthew 25:1-13

Background

In Matthew 24, Jesus was asked three questions by his disciples. He had just cried over Jerusalem and lamented their refusal to turn to God. He had said their house would be left unto them desolate. When he had finished, the disciples showed him the buildings of the temple, perhaps to show Israel's house was not desolate. He responded by saying not one stone would be left on another.

The disciples asked, "When will these things be? And what will be the sign of Your coming, and of the end of the age?" The remainder of chapter 24 is devoted to the Lord's answer. The disciples may have thought they were asking parts to one question. However, Jesus split his answer in two. The first part dealt with the time of the destruction of Jerusalem and the signs preceding that event. The second part dealt with the end of the world and the signs, or really the lack of signs, preceding it. He continued in chapter 25 by giving three parables about the kingdom and the end of time.

The Parable of the Ten Virgins

The Lord says, "Then the kingdom of heaven shall be likened unto ten virgins." In other words, the church is like ten virgins. Knowing the background, the word "then" clearly refers to the time of the Lord's return to earth.

Perhaps the most disturbing part of the parable comes when he goes on to say, "Now five of them were wise, and five were foolish." Thayer defines the word translated "foolish" as, "imprudent, without forethought or wisdom" (Matt. 7:24-27; Luke 12:13-21). Such is precisely the problem Jesus goes on to describe.

McGarvey says weddings in Christ's day "began with a feast in the house of the bride's father. After this the bridegroom led the bride to his own home, and it was the duty of his servants and household (of whom the ten virgins in this case were part) to honor him and the bride with an enthusiastic welcome." Edersheim explains, "The lamps consisted of a round receptacle for pitch or oil for the wick. This was placed in a hollow cup or deep saucer...which was fastened by a pointed end into a long wooden pole, on which it was borne aloft." Interestingly, he also noted Jewish authorities say there were usually ten such lamps in a wedding procession.

When the bridegroom delayed his coming, all nodded off to sleep. Around midnight, someone announced the groom was coming. The virgins began trimming their wicks and lighting their lamps to go out to meet him. The foolish, perhaps expecting to draw oil from a common supply, had brought no oil in their vessels in which the wick could be lain. They asked the wise to share. However, the wise declined saying they all might run out of oil before they could return to the house. They suggested the foolish go to merchants and buy oil.

While the foolish were out searching for oil, the bridegroom came. The wise entered into the wedding with him and the door was shut. Later, the foolish came knocking on the door. The Lord said he did not know them, in a favorable sense of the word. So, they were shut out of the wedding feast!

The Need for Preparation

The foolish virgins were expectantly awaiting the groom's coming. Their failure was in the area of preparation. The importance of preparation can be seen in the words of Jesus. "I must work the works of Him who sent Me while it is day; the night is coming when no one can work" (John 9:4). The rich fool in Luke 12 assumed he would live for many years, so he focused his efforts on providing for the flesh. Of course, he found out eternal provisions should take priority.

Another reason for preparation is found in 1 Peter 3:15. "But sanctify the Lord God in your hearts, and always be ready to give a defense to everyone who asks you a reason for the hope that is in you, with meekness and fear." Our readiness to preach the gospel can cause others to be ready to meet their God (2 Tim. 4:12; John 8:32; 17:17).

Some Things Cannot Be Borrowed

The foolish virgins wanted to rely on someone else's provisions to be ready. It is apparent some people expect to get to heaven based on the efforts of the whole church. Like the man who drives around looking for time still on a parking meter, they hope to park on the other fellow's quarter. This parable clearly shows such will not be possible in judgment. There are some things that simply cannot be borrowed.

Character is one example. Our parents' good character will not carry us through deceitful and cheating ways we might have. Obedience is another thing we cannot borrow from others. "So then each of us shall give account of himself to God" (Rom. 14:12; 2 Cor. 5:10).

Some are trying to live in a dream world where there are no consequences for immorality or lawlessness. However, Paul said, "Do not be deceived, God is not mocked; for whatever a man sows, that he will also reap. For he who sows to his flesh will of the flesh reap corruption, but he who sows to the Spirit will of the Spirit reap everlasting life" (Gal. 6:7-8).

Watch!

The Greeks pictured opportunity as a woman with long flowing hair in the front and bald in the back. Their thought was, if one does not grab her before she passes, there is nothing to grasp! Similarly, the Lord warned his followers to be watchful, or actively ready, because they do not know when his return will be. The Christian's opportunity to prepare for eternity will be past when this life ends at the second coming of the Lord.

The people around Noah abused over a hundred years of God's patience and failed to turn in time to be saved from destruction (2 Pet. 2:5). The rich man wanted Abraham to send Lazarus back to earth to warn his brothers. Abraham made it clear God has given those on earth the opportunity to learn and obey the truth. "If they do not hear Moses and the prophets, neither will they be persuaded though one rise from the dead" (Luke 16:31).

In recent years, numerous books have been written on the end of time. Often a date for the Lord's return is confidently set forth. Yet, the Lord himself made it plain that knowledge belongs exclusively to the Father. "But of that day and hour no one knows, no, not even the angels of heaven, but My Father only" (Matt. 24:36). To be truly watchful, we must be in a constant state of readiness. "See then that you walk circumspectly, not as fools but as wise, redeeming the time, because the days are evil" (Eph. 5:15-16). Because the wise virgins were ready, they had the joy of entering into the wedding feast. We must learn from them to be ready so that we can enter into the joys of heaven!

Discussion Questions

1. What questions was Jesus answering at the end of Matthew 24?

2. What does "foolish" mean? What did the five virgins do to be called such?

3. List some reasons you believe a Christian should continue preparing for eternity.

4. List some ways a Christian might try to "borrow oil" from his brethren.

5. What does the word "watch" mean? Why and for what should we be watching?

APPENDIX 1:
DOING THE FATHER'S WILL
Matthew 21:23-32

A Challenge to Christ's Authority

Jesus was walking in the temple area when the chief priests, scribes and elders confronted him (Mark 11:27). McGarvey says, "The Jewish Sanhedrin was generally designated by thus naming its three constituent parts." They came at this time to expose Jesus as one who had no authority to teach in or cleanse the temple. It was likely their hope to retake their place as the dominant religious force in the lives of the Jewish people. So, they asked him where he got his authority to do the things he did.

Jesus promised to answer if they would answer one question from him. He asked them whether John's baptism was from heaven or men. The problem for the members of the Sanhedrin was readily apparent. If they said John baptized under heaven's authority, he would ask them why they did not believe him. They, after all, had neither been baptized by him nor yielded to the one who came after him, that is, Jesus (John 1:67, 15, 32-34; 3:22-36; 10:40-42). If they said his authority was from men, they would be faced with the anger of the multitudes who believed him. So, they said they did not know. By so answering, they showed an unwillingness to yield to those empowered by God. Therefore, Jesus said he would not answer their question.

The Repentant Son

Jesus then told a parable about a father with two sons. The sons clearly represent the two classes of people among the Jews of Christ's day. The first class was that of the common Jewish people. In the parable, the father went to his first son and asked him to go into his vineyard and work. Though he was asked nicely, the son said, "I will not." The publicans and harlots had rejected God's will, as could be seen by their sinful lives. Like this son, they openly refused to do God's bidding.

Later, the first son repented and went to work in his father's vineyard. Similarly, the publicans and harlots had yielded to the teachings of John (Matt. 3:16). When Jesus passed through Jericho, he met a publican named Zacchaeus. This man determined to make restitution for any wrongs he had done the people and got to hear Jesus say, "Today salvation has come to this house, because he also is a son of Abraham" (Luke 19:1-10). In other words, the common folks repented and went when they heard God's word proclaimed.

The Son Who Refused To Do the Father's Will

The second son represents the chief priests, scribes and elders. When the father asked this son to go work in his vineyard, he immediately said he would. However, he never went. The Pharisees and others who considered themselves to be of the religious elite appeared to be anxious to do as God instructed. Yet, their lives showed disrespect for the Father's wishes (Matt. 3:7-12). Matthew 23 is a record of Jesus' scathing denunciation of their hypocritical response. They pretended to be quite religious while inwardly harboring vile sins.

Trapped By Their Own Response

When Jesus asked which of the sons did the will of the father, they had to say the first. Remember, Nathan used a parable to help David see his sin (2 Sam. 12:1-13). In fact, David condemned himself when he condemned the actions of the man in Nathan's parable. Similarly, the answer now given to the Lord exposes the actions of the Sanhedrin as opposed to those of the publicans and harlots. The religious leaders viewed the common people, especially the publicans and harlots, as having no special knowledge of God's will. They saw them as being ignorant of God's word. They clearly did not see their response as giving anyone credibility (John 7:45-49).

Refusing God's Spokesman

Despite all of this, the publicans and harlots had recognized John as a prophet. They had heeded his call to repentance. The religious leaders had failed to respond to God's call either before or after those they viewed as common sinners. The Pharisees demanded strict adherence to their demands for righteousness. John lived a righteous life. Yet, they refused to accept John as a spokesman in authority from God. The Lord knew such rejection showed the nature of their heart. There was no need for him to openly proclaim that his authority had come from God. They would reject him just as they had the baptizer.

God Still Calls Us to Work in His Vineyard

It is important readers today see the parable as still applicable. All men today must still be called to repentance (Luke 24:46-47; 1 Timothy 2:4). It is not enough to be a good moral person. Instead, each who would be saved must obey the will of the Father (Matt. 7:21). Just as the father asked his sons to work "today," we must respond now to the gospel call (Prov. 27:1; 2 Cor. 6:2). Further, it is possible to appear to be righteous to those around us without ever intending to do the will of the Father. The heart plays a critical role in our obedience (John 4:24; Prov. 23:7). Finally, we must recognize Jesus as God's spokesman for our time and yield to the message he brought down from the Father (Heb. 1:14). He made sure all truth was delivered by sending the Holy Spirit. We can know all that is necessary to have eternal life and be God like (John 16:13; 2 Pet. 1:3).

Discussion Questions

1. Tell the religious leaders' question to Jesus and his response.

2. What do the words and actions of the first son represent to you?

3. What do the words and actions of the second son represent to you?

4. What was the impact of Jesus' question at the end of the parable and the answer given by the religious leaders?

5. What other lessons do you find in this parable?

Gary C. Hampton

APPENDIX 2:
BEING FAITHFUL IN THE KINGDOM
Matthew 25:14-30

Stewards of the Lord's Goods

Literally, this parable begins, "For as a man going into another country...." Obviously, Jesus is again likening the church, or kingdom of heaven, to something his followers could understand. Notice, the man in the story gives his own servants a sum of money for which to care. They are his servants and the money is his. It is important each of us recognize that we and all we have belong to the Lord.

Paul told the people on Mars Hill, "For in Him we live and move and have our being, as also some of your own poets have said, 'For we are also His offspring'" (Acts 17:28). The Psalmist sang in behalf of the mighty God who is Lord, "For every beast of the forest is Mine, and the cattle on a thousand hills. I know all the birds of the mountains, and the wild beasts of the field are Mine" (50:10-11). These and other verses indicate we are simply stewards of things belonging to God, even including our own selves.

Good stewardship involves proper use of the things belonging to another. The servants in this parable were expected to gain even more, not just hold on to what they had. Paul described himself as a steward of God's mystery. Then, he said, "Moreover it is required in stewards that one be found faithful" (1 Cor. 4:12). A part of his faithful use of that mystery was entrusting it to others who would, in turn, place it in the safe keeping of others. "And the things that you have heard from me among many witnesses, commit these to faithful men who will be able to teach others also" (2 Tim. 2:2).

"Faithful Over a Few Things"

A talent was between 75 and 131 pounds, depending on which author one reads. It could have been gold or silver. Each man received a number of talents based on his lord's assessment of his ability to wisely use it to gain more. While their lord was away, the five and two talent men doubled what they had been given.

When the lord came back from his journey, he called his servants together to see what they had done with their trust. The five and two talent men both received the same words of commendation. "Well done, good and faithful servant; you were faithful over a few things, I will make you ruler over many things. Enter into the joy of your Lord" (Matt. 25:21, 23). The lord saw each man as having well used his trust. It did not matter that one earned five while the other earned only two. Instead, both were rewarded for faithful work.

God will judge each based on how he lived his life. Our concern need not be with what we have or do not have as compared to others. Instead, we must strive to faithfully use the Lord's trust! Our question should be, "What has the Lord given me and how can I use it to his glory?" Our goal should be to let our light shine so God can be glorified (Matt. 5:13-16).

"You Wicked and Lazy Servant"

The one talent man hid his money in a hole in the ground. When his master came back, he dug it up and brought it to him. Lightfoot sees three specific things which caused him to fail to please his master. First, he did not believe in himself. The Lord had evaluated his ability and given him what he was capable of appropriately using. Yet he did not believe he could use it wisely.

Second, he let fear keep him from working. Fear is a dangerous and immobilizing force. Jesus said the fearful would have their part in the second death, or hell (Rev. 21:8). Third, he envisioned his lord as a man looking for failures for which he could punish his servants. We need to realize God does not rejoice over our failures. Remember, God is love. His love for lost mankind was so great he sent his Son to die in their stead (John 3:16-17; Rom. 5:68; 1 John 4:7-11). Out of that true love comes a willingness to be longsuffering, kind, not rejoice in our sins, but rejoice in our obedience to the truth (1 Cor. 13:4-8).

Outer Darkness

The lord in Jesus' parable describes the one talent man as wicked and lazy. He knew his master would want him to work with what he had been given. Still, he failed to seize his opportunities for work. Do we really have to wonder what the Lord thinks of the church today? We are in the middle of a technical revolution. We can communicate around the globe in a matter of minutes. Through television and radio, we can reach multiplied millions with the gospel at any moment. Many of our friends and neighbors have heard more about our lawns than they have about Jesus. How will the Lord describe our efforts? What will our reward be?

Our answer to these questions may give us a different view of the judgment against the one talent man. "And cast the unprofitable servant into the outer darkness. There shall be weeping and gnashing of teeth" (Matt. 25:30). This is in stark contrast to the "joy of your Lord" which was given to both the five talent man and the two talent man. If we would have joy and avoid the place where crying and teeth grinding is incessant, we must put what the Lord has given us to use!

Discussion Questions

1. Over what things has God given you stewardship?

2. What could you do to faithfully use the things God has provided?

3. What lessons do you learn from the two commendations given by the Lord?

4. List reasons you think the one talent man might have hidden the money.

5. What is "outer darkness"? How should we live if we do not want to go there?

APPENDIX 3:
THE KINGDOM AND THE JUDGMENT
Matthew 25:31-46

"All the Nations Will Be Gathered Before Him"

Though some have taught to the contrary, Jesus plainly said everyone in the grave would be raised. "Do not marvel at this; for the hour is coming in which all who are in the graves will hear His voice and come forth--those who have done good, to the resurrection of life, and those who have done evil, to the resurrection of condemnation" (John 5:28-29). The parable of the judgment pictures what will happen following that resurrection.

Jesus said he would be seated on his glorious throne, where he has been seated since the days of the new birth began (Matt. 19:28). Peter told the crowd assembled on Pentecost that our Lord was then seated on his throne (Acts 2:32-36; 1 Cor. 15:24-28). All nations, that is every person from those nations, will come before the throne. Jesus will divide those people into two groups, the sheep, who are representative of those who accepted his leading, and the goats, representing those who would not be led but had to be driven. The sheep will be placed on the right hand because that is the place of honor, while the goats will be on the left where, according to tradition, those condemned in their trials before the Sanhedrin stood (Matthew 25:31-33).

"Come, You Blessed of My Father"

Even before the world began, God planned a kingdom for the redeemed to inherit. "But we speak the wisdom of God in a mystery, the hidden wisdom which God ordained before the ages for our glory" (1 Cor. 2:7; Eph. 1:4, 9-14). In the judgment, the King, Christ Jesus our Lord, will invite the faithful to come into that kingdom (Matt. 25:34).

Jesus then listed six separate acts of service done for others as the reason those on the right hand will be invited (Matt. 25:35-36). McGarvey says, "The acts here enumerated indicate more than a mere outlay of money. They are not such as are the offspring of impulse, but such as call for the sacrifice of time, strength, sympathy, etc., and clearly demonstrate the fullness of the Christian life." True love for the brethren, without which one cannot claim to love God, will motivate one to act in their behalf. "But whoever has this world's goods, and sees his brother in need, and shuts up his heart from him, how does the love of God abide in him? My little children, let us not love in word or in tongue, but in deed and in truth" (1 John 3:17-18; 4:20-21). Only an actively loving faith is truly alive (1 Cor. 13:1-3; James 2:14-17).

Jesus portrayed those bidden to enter asking when they had seen the Lord in such situations and helped him. He said he will respond by saying, "Assuredly, I say to you, inasmuch as you did it to one of the least of these My brethren, you did it to Me" (Matt. 25:37-40; compare Mark 9:41). This is reminiscent of the Lord asking Saul of Tarsus why he persecuted him, when in fact he had been persecuting the church (Acts 9:4). Jesus so closely identifies with the members of his body that to hurt them or help them is to do the same to him!

"Depart from Me, You Cursed"

Just as surely as God has prepared a kingdom for his own, he has prepared an everlasting fire for the devil and his angels. It is sad to hear the King saying some men will be condemned to that fire because they have not ministered to those in need. In case the point was not understood before, we find Jesus telling those on the left hand that they will not enter in because they failed to tend him when they saw him in need. Like those on the right hand, they will ask when they saw him in such a condition and did not attend to him. His response was, "Assuredly, I say to you, inasmuch as you did not do it to one of the least of these, you did not do it to Me" (Matt. 25:41-45).

In verse 41, hell was described as an everlasting fire. In verse 46, he says it will be a place of everlasting punishment. McGarvey says, "The word 'punishment' expresses misery and suffering purposely inflicted." He also noted the condemnation of the wicked will be just as long in its duration as the reward of the righteous. There is no doctrine of a second chance taught in this parable of our Lord. It is imperative that we all prepare to stand before his judgment seat today!

Note: Two other parables were told by the Lord in explaining the need to be prepared for his unexpected return. These can be found in Appendix 2 and Appendix 3.

Discussion Questions

1. Where is Jesus today? Give scriptures to support your answer.

2. Who do you think will be raised to appear before Christ's judgment seat and why?

3. How long has God been preparing an inheritance for the redeemed? Who will be told to come in?

4. How long will hell last? What will it be like? For whom was it intended? Who will also have to go there?

5. What type of relationship does Christ have with individual Christians? Why do you think so?

BIBLIOGRAPHY

Edersheim. *The Life and Times of Jesus the Messiah*. MacDonald
    Publishing Company, n.d.

Lightfoot, Neil R. *Lessons from the Parables*. Grand Rapids: Baker
    Book House, 1965.

McGarvey, J. W. and Philip Y. Pendleton. *The Fourfold Gospel: A
    Harmony of the Four Gospels*. Cincinnati: The Standard
    Publishing Foundation, n.d.

45004362R00060

Made in the USA
Charleston, SC
12 August 2015